THE AMERICAN REVOLUTION
FIGHTING FOR FREEDOM

Torrey Maloof

Consultants

Katie Blomquist, M.Ed.
Fairfax County Public Schools

Nicholas Baker, Ed.D.
Supervisor of Curriculum
and Instruction
Colonial School District, DE

Publishing Credits

Rachelle Cracchiolo, M.S.Ed., *Publisher*
Conni Medina, M.A.Ed., *Managing Editor*
Emily R. Smith, M.A.Ed., *Series Developer*
Diana Kenney, M.A.Ed., NBCT, *Content Director*
Johnson Nguyen, *Multimedia Designer*
Torrey Maloof, *Editor*

Image Credits: pp.2–3, 4, 5, 6, 7, 10, 11, 12, 13 (top), 18, 23, 26, 28–29, 29 North Wind Picture Archives; pp. 5, 6, 20–21, 24, 26 Granger, NYC; p.8 LOC [DIG-ppmsca-05478]; p.13 (bottom) Jessi Hagood; p.15 LOC [LC-USZCN4-159]; p.16 SuperStock/Alamy; p.17 Universal History Archive/UIG/Bridgeman Images; p.21 Yale University Art Gallery; p.22 Chronicle/Alamy; p.22 Library of Congress; p.27 Wikimedia Commons/Public Domain; all other images from iStock and/or Shutterstock.

Library of Congress Cataloging-in-Publication Data

Names: Maloof, Torrey, author.
Title: The American Revolution: fighting for freedom / Torrey Maloof.
Description: Huntington Beach, CA : Teacher Created Materials, 2017. |
    Includes index. | Audience: Grades 4-6.?
Identifiers: LCCN 2015051145 (print) | LCCN 2016010646 (ebook) | ISBN
    9781493830794 (pbk.) | ISBN 9781480756816 (eBook)
Subjects: LCSH: United States--History--Revolution,
    1775-1783--Causes--Juvenile literature. | United
    States--History--Revolution, 1775-1783--Juvenile literature.
Classification: LCC E210 .M33 2017 (print) | LCC E210 (ebook) | DDC
    973.3/11--dc23
LC record available at http://lccn.loc.gov/2015051145

Teacher Created Materials
5301 Oceanus Drive
Huntington Beach, CA 92649-1030
http://www.tcmpub.com
ISBN 978-1-4938-3079-4

Table of Contents

War Is Coming!

"Listen my children and you shall hear
Of the midnight ride of Paul Revere."

The poet Henry Wadsworth Longfellow wrote these lines. Before this poem was published, the story of Revere's now-famous ride was not well known. While the poem is not entirely accurate, it does bring to light an important piece of American history.

Revere's ride occurred right on the brink of the American Revolution. At that time, the tension between the British and the colonists had reached its peak. Colonists were fed up with all the taxes. They were tired of the restrictions placed on them by the British. They wanted to be treated fairly. War was looming on the horizon. It was **inevitable**.

Paul Revere's famous ride in 1775

Colonists discuss their discontent.

The **Patriots** were colonists who wanted to break free from Great Britain's rule. They were preparing for war. **Militias** (mi-LISH-uhz) were training. Strategies were being created. Weapons were being gathered. The British soon caught wind of these plots. British soldiers prepared to leave Boston. They headed toward Concord and Lexington. Their mission was to take the colonists' weapons and arrest **traitorous** troublemakers. But colonists were one step ahead of the British. They devised a plan—a warning system.

Sons of Liberty

The British tried to arrest Patriot leaders, such as Samuel Adams and John Hancock, who encouraged colonists to fight for freedom. They had formed the Sons of Liberty, a group of store owners and workers who fought against unfair treatment by the British.

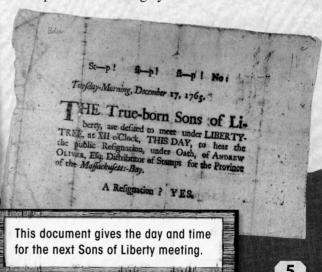

St—p! St—p! St—p! No!

Tuesday-Morning, December 17, 1765.

THE True-born Sons of Liberty, are desired to meet under LIBERTY-TREE, at XII o'Clock, THIS DAY, to hear the public Resignation, under Oath, of ANDREW OLIVER, Esq; Distributor of Stamps for the Province of the Massachusetts-Bay.

A Resignation ? YES.

This document gives the day and time for the next Sons of Liberty meeting.

Revere had some of his men watching the British soldiers in Boston. When the soldiers left, the men were to climb to the steeple of Old North Church. If the British were traveling by land, they were to light one lantern in the steeple. If they were taking the shortcut and traveling by sea, the men were to light two lanterns. As Longfellow famously wrote in his poem, "One if by land, two if by sea."

On the night of April 18, 1775, two lanterns lit the steeple. Revere began his ride at 10 p.m. It was time to warn everyone that the British were coming! He rode toward Lexington. This was where Samuel Adams and John Hancock were hiding. He didn't want these Patriot leaders to be captured by the British. He arrived just after midnight and warned the men and the militia there.

Two lanterns light Old North Church.

one of the lanterns used to signal Paul Revere

Paul Revere warns colonists that the British are coming.

Mythbuster

Many people think that Revere shouted "The British are coming!" on his ride. But, they aren't correct! Revere tried to be discreet. And, colonists thought of themselves as British!

Next, Revere and two other men jumped on their horses and took off toward Concord. They warned everyone they saw along the way. The British captured all three men before they could reach Concord, but the damage was done. The colonial militias had been warned. When the British arrived on April 19, they found armed angry colonists waiting for them. They were ready to fight!

Paul Revere

And So It Begins

Captain John Parker was a veteran of the French and Indian War and the leader of a group of *minutemen*. They were called *minutemen* because they could be ready to fight with a minute's notice. Most of these men were farmers and did not have battle experience.

Parker received the message spread by Revere and his men. Parker knew the British were coming. He assembled his men and told them, "Stand your ground. Don't fire unless fired upon, but if they mean to have a war, let it begin here." The spot where Parker said these words in Lexington is where the American Revolution began.

the Battle of Lexington in 1775

No one knows who fired the first shot. When the battle at Lexington ended, eight colonists were dead. Only one British soldier was injured. But the fighting was not over. The British marched on to Concord. Most of the weapons the British were looking for had already been hidden elsewhere by the colonists. The few weapons the British did find they burned. Colonists worried the British were going to burn the whole town. The hundreds of minutemen who assembled in Concord charged the British soldiers. The British fired. The minutemen fired back. The British **retreated**. The minutemen followed and kept shooting.

North Bridge in Concord, Massachusetts

statue of a minuteman

First Shots

The first shots in Concord were fired at North Bridge. In 1837, a poet by the name of Ralph Waldo Emerson wrote a poem about this moment in American history. The poem is titled "Concord Hymn."

During the battles of Lexington and Concord, the Americans fought against the best army in the world. The British were well trained. They had military experience. Yet the Americans stood their ground. The colonists killed or wounded around 250 British soldiers. There were about 90 **casualties** on the American side.

George Washington takes command of the Continental army.

He Looked the Part

Washington's stature made him look like a leader. He was tall. He had broad shoulders. Abigail Adams once said, "He has a dignity that forbids familiarity, mixed with an easy affability that creates love and reverence."

In Philadelphia, the **Continental Congress** had a new priority. The war had begun. All of the militias needed to be united to form one army. But who would lead that army? He had to be a strong and brave man. He needed military experience. He had to be respected. And he needed to be committed to America's fight for independence. The Congress chose George Washington.

Washington fought in the French and Indian War. He was a leader in the Virginia colony. And he was fully devoted to the Patriot cause. However, Washington was not sure he was the right man for the job. He doubted his abilities. He told his friend, Patrick Henry, that he was concerned becoming commander of the American army would ruin his reputation. Yet, he accepted the position. He bought books on how to lead and organize a large army. He studied. He trained. He wanted to win the war.

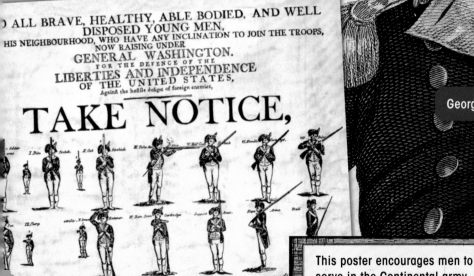

George Washington

This poster encourages men to serve in the Continental army.

The Battle of Bunker Hill

In the dark of night on June 16, American troops received orders to march to Bunker Hill. It was just outside Boston. On the hill, they would build **fortifications**. They were going to fight the advancing British soldiers from there. But the men set up their defenses on Breed's Hill instead.

The Americans quickly built walls and **barricades** to protect against British fire. In the morning, British soldiers marched toward the hill. The Americans knew they had limited **ammunition**. They were told "Don't fire 'til you see the whites of their eyes!" The Americans waited. They were nervous and frightened.

The British marched up the hill. When they got close enough, the Americans fired. Eventually, they forced the British to retreat. The British reorganized their troops and marched up the hill again. The Americans attacked and forced the British soldiers back down the hill a second time. But on the third attempt made by the British, the Americans ran out of ammunition. They were forced to flee. They lost the battle. The British took control of the hills surrounding Boston and the peninsula. But once again, the Americans felt proud. They had held off the British, even if it was just for a short time.

This British map shows the positions of Breed's Hill and Bunker Hill reversed.

Wrong Place

No one knows if the troops chose Breed's Hill on purpose or got confused in the dark. Either way, the battle is known as the Battle of Bunker Hill. There is even a plaque at the top of Breed's Hill that says so.

BREED'S HILL
SITE OF THE
BATTLE OF BUNKER HILL
FOUGHT JUNE 17 1775
ALTHOUGH ORDERS WERE ISSUED BY THE
COMMITTEE OF SAFETY
TO SEIZE AND FORTIFY BUNKER HILL
THE COLONIAL OFFICERS AFTER CONSULTATION
FORTIFIED THIS HILL ON JUNE 16, 1775

Crossing the Delaware

On July 4, 1776, the Congress adopted the Declaration of Independence. The colonists had been fighting the British for over a year. The Declaration gave the soldiers a clear vision of what they were fighting for—independence. It motivated them. It raised their spirits. But by the time winter arrived later that year, the troops were exhausted and downtrodden. They needed another inspirational event. They needed their first big victory in battle. Washington knew this. He devised a plan.

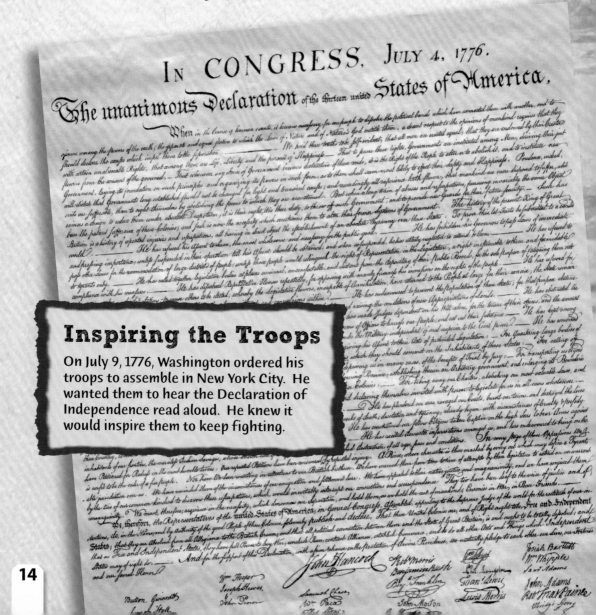

Inspiring the Troops

On July 9, 1776, Washington ordered his troops to assemble in New York City. He wanted them to hear the Declaration of Independence read aloud. He knew it would inspire them to keep fighting.

Washington and his troops cross the Delaware River.

Washington wanted to launch a surprise attack. They would surprise a group of soldiers in Trenton, New Jersey. The group had built their winter camp there. The attack would take place on Christmas Day. He picked this day because he knew the enemy soldiers would be tired from celebrating the holiday. It was a good plan. But to get to Trenton, Washington's men had to cross the frozen and treacherous Delaware River. It was not an easy task. Yet 2,400 troops made it through ice and sleet to the other side. The surprise attack was a success. They won the battle! Washington's plan worked. The victory raised the spirits of the troops. And it also raised the spirits of Americans throughout the 13 colonies.

The Turning Point

British General John Burgoyne (buhr-GOYN) left Canada. He marched toward New York. And he brought 7,200 troops with him! His mission was to isolate New England and New York. He thought if he could cut off these colonies from the rest, then the war would soon be over. Burgoyne's troops met American forces near Saratoga, New York, on September 19, 1777. This was the first of two battles. The British won this battle. But they suffered more losses. Almost 600 British soldiers died. Yet there were only about 150 American casualties.

General John Burgoyne

Famous Franklin

Benjamin Franklin was sent to France in October of 1776. Franklin was quite popular in France, but he was unable to secure an alliance until the victory at Saratoga.

Burgoyne wanted to wait until more troops arrived before engaging in another battle. But, **reinforcements** never came. He decided to move forward. On October 7, the British launched their second attack. American General Horatio Gates and his men held firm. They forced the British troops back. Then, they surrounded them. By October 17, Burgoyne surrendered.

These two battles were a major turning point in the war. Why? Because this victory brought an **alliance**. After these battles, the French decided to help America in the war effort. They sent troops and supplies. They sent ships and money, too. Thanks to France's help, American forces grew much stronger. Without their help, the war may have ended much differently.

General Burgoyne surrenders at Saratoga.

Valley Forge

The American troops were exhausted. Many were sick. They had little food. Their uniforms were in tatters and some had no shoes. The ground was covered in snow, the wind was icy, and the river was frozen solid. This was the grisly scene at Valley Forge.

In the fall of 1777, British forces captured Philadelphia. It was a big blow to Washington to lose the capital city. By this time, his troops had suffered many losses, and now they were about to face a harsh winter at a camp 18 miles outside of Philadelphia.

American troops at Valley Forge

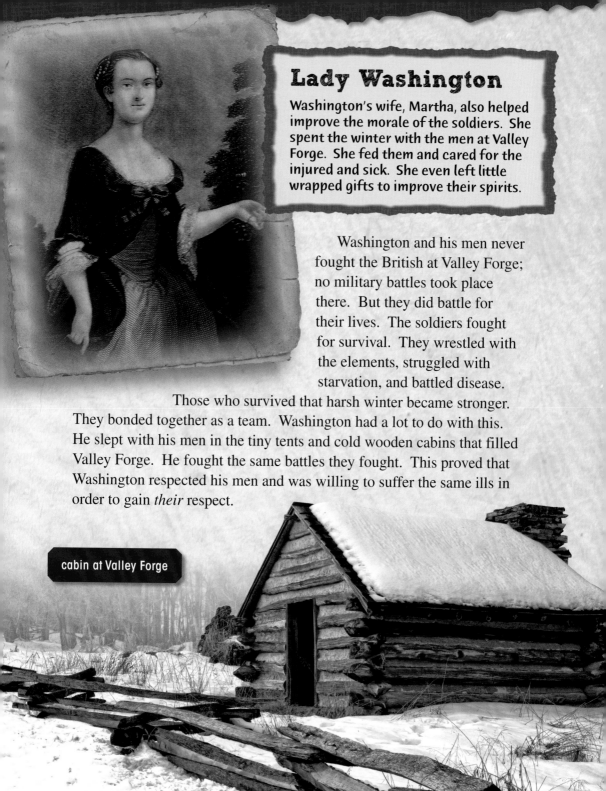

Lady Washington

Washington's wife, Martha, also helped improve the morale of the soldiers. She spent the winter with the men at Valley Forge. She fed them and cared for the injured and sick. She even left little wrapped gifts to improve their spirits.

Washington and his men never fought the British at Valley Forge; no military battles took place there. But they did battle for their lives. The soldiers fought for survival. They wrestled with the elements, struggled with starvation, and battled disease. Those who survived that harsh winter became stronger. They bonded together as a team. Washington had a lot to do with this. He slept with his men in the tiny tents and cold wooden cabins that filled Valley Forge. He fought the same battles they fought. This proved that Washington respected his men and was willing to suffer the same ills in order to gain *their* respect.

cabin at Valley Forge

Something else happened that winter at Valley Forge. The soldiers became more disciplined and learned better fighting techniques. This was due in large part to a man named Baron Friedrich von Steuben (STOO-buhn). He was from **Prussia**. He was a captain in the military there. Benjamin Franklin met him in France. He suggested that Washington use von Steuben to help train the American army. And that's just what Washington did.

Von Steuben arrived at Valley Forge in February of 1778. He could not believe how dirty the camp conditions were. One of the first things he did was move the **latrines** away from where the soldiers were living. This helped the soldiers stay clean. He also moved the kitchens to the opposite side of the camp to keep the food away from the latrines. He then organized the camp into companies and regiments.

Baron von Steuben trains the Continental army at Valley Forge.

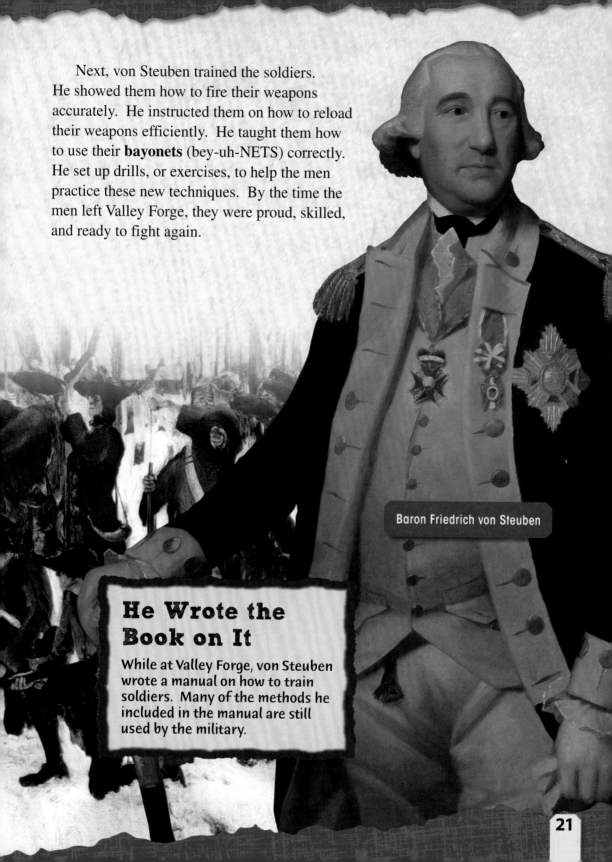

Next, von Steuben trained the soldiers. He showed them how to fire their weapons accurately. He instructed them on how to reload their weapons efficiently. He taught them how to use their **bayonets** (bey-uh-NETS) correctly. He set up drills, or exercises, to help the men practice these new techniques. By the time the men left Valley Forge, they were proud, skilled, and ready to fight again.

Baron Friedrich von Steuben

He Wrote the Book on It

While at Valley Forge, von Steuben wrote a manual on how to train soldiers. Many of the methods he included in the manual are still used by the military.

Sneaky Spies

Fighting wasn't the only strategy used in the American Revolution. Both sides engaged in sneaky methods in an attempt to win the war. The most famous and effective group of spies was the Culper Spy Ring. These men and women were Patriots. They risked their own lives to secretly gather information from the British. Then, they covertly passed the information along to General Washington. It was dangerous work. If they were caught, they would be hanged!

In 1778, Washington asked for a spy network to be formed. He placed Major Benjamin Tallmadge (TAL-mij) in charge of the secret operation. This became the Culper Spy Ring. First, Tallmadge needed men and women he could trust. So, he chose his childhood friends. Then, they were all given code names. They also wrote in code. And they used invisible ink! They even hung laundry on clotheslines to signal each other.

Culper Spy Ring code

Major Benjamin Tallmadge

The ring of spies gathered information that helped Washington win the war. Once, they alerted Washington about the British plan to attack the French who were en route to help the Americans. They also gathered information that led to the downfall of the American traitor Benedict Arnold. None of Tallmadge's spies were ever caught!

> **This coded message told Americans what the British troops were planning.**

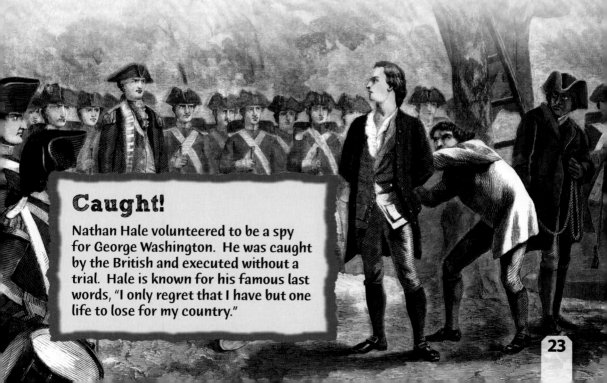

CLINTON HAS SENT A SECRET EXPEDITION UP

THE HUDSON TO INTERCEPT WASHINGTON.

Caught!

Nathan Hale volunteered to be a spy for George Washington. He was caught by the British and executed without a trial. Hale is known for his famous last words, "I only regret that I have but one life to lose for my country."

Siege and Surrender

British General Cornwallis brought his troops to Yorktown, Virginia, in August 1781. The plan was to take over Virginia. Yorktown was by the sea on Chesapeake Bay. Cornwallis was waiting for more troops and supplies to arrive by ship. Then, he would begin fighting. But Washington and his army were one step ahead of Cornwallis.

George Washington at Yorktown

Washington accepts Cornwallis's sword.

Washington knew French ships were on their way to Yorktown. They could block the supplies and troops Cornwallis was waiting for. They could also stop the British stationed at Yorktown from leaving by sea once the fighting started. But Washington needed troops on land. His men and French soldiers were in Rhode Island. That was 500 miles away. Would they be able to make the trek in time? Yes, they would!

Called in Sick

Cornwallis did not surrender to Washington in person. He claimed he was too sick to attend. Instead, he sent his second in command to offer Washington his sword in surrender.

The American and French soldiers dug trenches and set up their cannons outside of Yorktown. Then, they attacked! The British woke that morning to find themselves surrounded. They were trapped! The fighting lasted three weeks. Then, Cornwallis surrendered. By October 19, 1781, it was all over. The British could not recover from this battle. America went on to win the war. In 1783, the United States of America officially became an independent nation.

13 Clocks

In 1818, John Adams wrote a letter. It was a very insightful letter about the American Revolution. He said there had been *two* revolutions. There was the one that involved guns and fighting—the war. But there was another one in the "minds and hearts of the people" of the 13 colonies. There was an **awakening**. They knew it was time for a change. They wanted to govern themselves. They needed a government based on equality, one in which justice ruled, not a king.

This badge from the French Revolution was given to military school students.

John Adams

LIBERTÉ
CONSTITUTION
CONSTITUTION
LIBERTÉ

Liberty, Equality, Fraternity

The American Revolution proved that old systems could be replaced and new governments started. Other countries also sought liberty. In their 1787 revolution, the French declared, "Liberty, Equality, Fraternity."

Adams wrote that *this* revolution was the first time in history that such a "difficult **enterprise**" was accomplished in "so short a time and by such simple means." He described the 13 colonies uniting under one cause as "thirteen clocks [that] were made to strike together." He said it was a "perfection of **mechanism**."

These "13 clocks striking as one" were heard around the world. It inspired future **democracies**. It sparked a movement to end slavery. It inspired women to fight for their rights. Change was on the horizon for the world at large.

French citizens revolt during the French Revolution.

Code It!

During the American Revolution, spies were used by both sides to gather secret information. This helped them plan their next move. Spies used many tricks and codes.

Imagine you are a spy during the war. You need to share important information with General George Washington. Create a secret code that you can use to hide the information. Then, write a letter to Washington using your code.

Give your letter and your code to a friend. See if he or she can decode your message!

An American woman serves tea to gather information from a British officer.

This cipher alphabet was used by Patriots to send messages during the American Revolution.

Glossary

alliance—a relationship in which people agree to work together

ammunition—bullets and shells that are shot from weapons

awakening—becoming aware of something

barricades—temporary walls, fences, or similar structures that are built to prevent people from entering a place or area

bayonets—long knives that are attached to the end of rifles and are often used as weapons in battle

casualties—people who are hurt or killed during an accident or war

Continental Congress—meeting of colonial leaders to decide how to deal with Great Britain and to decide on laws

democracies—forms of government in which people choose leaders by voting

enterprise—a project or activity that involves many people and that is often difficult

fortifications—military structures built for defense to protect against enemy attacks

inevitable—something that is impossible to avoid or that is sure to happen

latrines—outdoor toilets that are usually holes dug in the ground

mechanism—a piece of machinery

militias—groups of regular citizens trained in military combat and willing to fight and defend their country

Patriots—people who supported American independence from Great Britain

Prussia—a former kingdom that is known today as Germany

reinforcements—people and supplies that are sent to help an army or military force

retreated—moved away from an enemy because the enemy is winning or has won the battle

traitorous—relating to the act of betraying one's own country by helping an enemy

Index

Your Turn!

TO ALL BRAVE, HEALTHY, ABLE BODIED, AND WE
DISPOSED YOUNG MEN,
IN THIS NEIGHBOURHOOD, WHO HAVE ANY INCLINATION TO JOIN THE TRO
NOW RAISING UNDER
GENERAL WASHINGTON.
FOR THE DEFENCE OF THE
LIBERTIES AND INDEPENDENCE
OF THE UNITED STATES,
Against the hostile designs of foreign enemies,

TAKE NOTICE,

Join Now!

This is a poster from the American Revolution. It urges men to join the Continental army to help the United States win the war. Create your own poster. Try to convince people to either join the Patriot cause or to stay loyal to the British. Which side will you choose?